One Decision Investing

Buffett's

strategy for
WEALTH

Law Steeple MBA
The Miracle of Compounding

IAN Books

An IAN Books paperback

Published by
IAN Books
41 Watchung Plaza, B242
Montclair, NJ 07042

Cover photo: Obama & Buffett by Pete Souza

Special sales for educational use by nonprofits.
IANBooksEditor@yahoo.com

ISBN-13: 9781723529177

ISBN-10: 1723529176

IAN Books at <u>Amazon.com</u>

Wealth Without Wall Street:
Buy Direct -- Avoid the Commissions, Fees, Loads

The Insiders' Guides to Buying Discount Financial Services:
Buy Direct and Save $3,000 Every Year

Drop Your Insurance:
Buy Only What You Need

Create Financial Freedom Using Your Wealth Reserve™:
Fix your financial life

The Simple Financial Life:
How to get what you want without going into debt and living paycheck to paycheck

Build Wealth Without Extra Money or Time:
You don't need to budget or get an extra job

Tax-FREE Retirement:
Use the tax code for lifetime income free of tax

The Working Millionaire:
$2,000,000 Tax-FREE Wealth Reserve ™ Self-insure Self-fund

Build Your Own $2,000,000 Tax-FREE Wealth Reserve™:
Self-insure Self-fund your lifestyle

Stop wasting $3,000 every year:
101
financial products ***NOT*** to buy and why

One Decision

Wall Street is wrong

Warren Buffett, the most successful investor of our lifetime, just proved that there is only One Decision you need to make to reach your lifetime goals. He bet $1 million on a One Decision strategy against a Wall Street guru with 4 different strategies.
He beat them all. It is simple, he says.

"A very low-cost index is going to beat a majority of the amateur-managed money or professionally-managed money"

A recent study of investments showed that when you pay less, you earn more. Another study showed that over a lifetime of investing, you may give up 63% of your potential nest egg by paying just 2%.
Buffett thinks the wealthy don't follow his advice because they think they are smarter than everyone else. But a business person realizes that it is impossible to pick the next Apple or Google. Just like most people know they will not win the lottery no matter how many tickets they buy.
What most people don't realize is that it is the Miracle of Compounding that makes and keeps the rich rich. Buffett says:

My wealth has come from a combination of living in America, some lucky genes
and
compound interest.

You can earn $1,000,000 with $250 a month over time in a low-cost index or just $208,000 with an advisor account averaging 3.79%. So why don't most of us take Buffett's advice and use index funds? The reason: we never learned about them. No one taught us. Our schools never taught us. Most of our parents couldn't teach us either. Even now pre-retirees lack vital knowledge to fix their shortfall.
The *One Decision* strategy is not used because we never learned that the stocks in the most common index are the safest investment we can own for the LONG-TERM. We never learned that bank accounts are only safe for the SHORT TERM. We never learned that the average return of a low-cost index of the largest

500 stocks is over 11% over time. We never learned that this is not just a guess by academics but a reality available to everyone no matter how much or little we have to invest.

Look at the oldest and most successful index fund anyone can buy: Vanguard 500 Index Fund. The cost is 85% LESS than comparable funds from brokers. You own very profitable companies like Apple Google and Amazon. Since 1976, you would have earned 11% a year. If you had invested just $250 a month in this one fund since '76 you would have about $1,111,000. Compounding earned $1,012,000. You spent $99,000.

Your account *balance* would have gone up 32% and down 37% but you still would have reached your goal because you did not sell your asset: *shares*. Not many brokers or money managers could have helped you there—only Buffett has consistently beaten the index over time with about 19% a year since 1965.

This is your **One Decision** investment move—just have the fund trustee at Vanguard or other low-cost fund debit $250 a month from your checking automatically, and voilà, $1 million. You do nothing else if you want to reach your money targets over time. If you or your advisor sell or stop buying *shares* you lose the compounding factor. If your salesperson takes any fees greater than 0.04% (Vanguard drops your fee 70% with a $10,000 balance), you are giving them your money for no benefit to you.

The very profitable financial industry has kept this strategy secret for over 30 years. Only 5 states may make this information available to high schoolers in a course. In the past, you had to use a stock broker to buy mutual fund *shares*. They required a large purchase. And the brokers had to keep moving your money around to generate commissions and fees to earn a living.

Vanguard changed all that. John Bogle, the founder, realized that without high costs, investors could earn more by paying less. Vanguard sells fund *shares* directly to us and the *shares* are bought at cost since the fund is owned by us. It is an actual co-op like farm co-ops, buying large quantities of supplies for farmers without a owner's profit.

We don't need expensive brokers, advisors or agents to create an efficient financial plan. In fact, their high-cost products can take over HALF of our accumulations. All we need is TIME and a plan.

We buy only what we need at discount prices. We don't pay

high costs: <u>fees, commissions, charges, expense ratios, bookkeeping, or trading</u>. Over time, the stock market provides 10-12% returns a year. Now we don't have to pay 1-3% a year in order to grow our money. We don't give up over 50% of our earnings:

> $3,000 per year @11%   for 33 years = $1,111,000
> $3,000 per year @11-1% for 33 years = $778,768
> $3,000 per year @11-2% for 33 years = $613,805
> $3,000 per year @11-3% for 33 years = $486,634

With ***One Decision***, we can earn 11% on our long-term money and end up with a million dollars or more with one phone call. We do not need an advisor or learn how to pick stocks. That is the fastest way to ***lose*** money. The average advisor-assisted investor earned just <u>3.79%</u> instead of the market rate of 11%. Dalbar's <u>QAIB</u>.

'Playing the market' by trading stocks and trying to time the market gyrations is the <u>Loser's Game</u> according to research.

We can't afford hedge funds, offshore tax shelters, and expensive Wall Street money managers <u>taking 1-3% a year</u>. We are not as experienced as Mr Buffett. A plain market index fund beat <u>92-95%</u> of the returns of "professional" managers, including <u>hedge funds</u>. Stock picking by geniuses only works for a short time.

To earn more, we pay as little as we can. We own stocks of companies with <u>certain characteristics</u>. We Pay Less; Earn More.

Instead of trading stocks, we buy more of them when the price is low and fewer when it is high. No one can time the market successfully in the long run.

We don't pay Wall Street owners the <u>$1.3 Trillion per year revenues</u> they take from clients now. If you think you need financial help, pay for a one-time session from a certified planner, not quarterly fees taking 1-2% of your account every year.

Your current advisor is costing you real money. The <u>average return for managed accounts is 3.79%</u>. A low-cost index fund provides <u>11%</u>. You are giving up <u>63% of your total potential earnings</u>. You can do better on your own with the One Decision strategy. Do you really think an expert at selling knows anything about what will happen to a security or the market in the next hour, week or year?

Low-cost stock mutual funds are our ***only*** viable long-term asset over time. <u>Other assets have lower or more volatile returns</u>. If you have 10 years until you need the money, stocks give you the power to beat inflation as well as all other investments over time.

Selling and buying stocks kills **compounding** the Buffett strategy for wealth: Vanguard's 500 index return: 11.02% since 1976. All we have to do is buy and keep buying low-cost funds.

I will show you how you can grow your investing dollar to a $ million or more. An hour online or by phone is all you need to set up the account. We use a special investment account to eliminate all future taxes on this money too. It is IRS-approved for workers.

You have a TAX-FREE account with no brokerage fees or commissions. You keep ALL your hard-earned money and earnings, including the capital gains taxes others have to pay. The less you pay the more you keep. And no taxes!

The wealthy have figured out how to avoid taxes. For instance, Warren Buffett, with $90 billions, pays only 17% **total** tax: http://www.youtube.com/watch?v=Cu5B-2LoC4s; Mitt Romney only **14%**; John Kerry only **13%** and Apple just **9.8%**. Buffett found that his staff pays **32.9%**—DOUBLE their rate!

You set up a tax-FREE account with the largest mutual fund company. You will have that company's trustee invest your automatic bank debit once a month. You do nothing else—No trading; No market timing; No speculation. It's *TIME, not timing*.

Bogle created the first consumer index fund. You do not need to try to pick the "needle" in the haystack, he says. The chance of your advisor identifying the next Apple or Google is 1 in 19,000. Because there are so many variables that we can't determine as a company grows, it is almost impossible to pick, in advance, the one that beats the market *over time*. We can pick the TIME we spend in the market not the one blockbuster stock.

Warren Buffett shared his strategy of building assets. He buys, on sale, stocks of companies we all use and holds them "forever." We acknowledge that no one can pick the next Amazon, Apple or Google so we buy and hold low-cost funds with the stocks of companies that have the 'longevity gene.'

We use the One Decision strategy to provide wealth for you and your family. We pay less and so earn more.

Avoid income taxes

The One Decision strategy relies on Bogle and Buffett. But the One Decision strategy works even better when we make our account tax-FREE.

The wealthy have ways we don't have to avoid taxes. Consider the examples above: Buffett pays just **17%**, Romney **14%**, Kerry **13%** and Apple **9.8%**. Most of the top 1% pay far less tax than the average American in terms of income.

If the average middle-class <u>family earns $85,000</u>, they pay about 14% federal, 13% SS/Med/UC/Health, 10% <u>state/local</u>, 4% sales/excise, or over 30% <u>total taxes</u>. As Buffett said, "<u>I pay 17.7% total tax. My office staff pays 32.9%.</u>" This does not include pension, insurance and other deductions most Americans also pay.

This is why the wealthy avoid taxes with their own businesses and various <u>tax-advantaged</u> vehicles. In order to become and stay wealthy, people need to have money to invest. The average family has little extra money to build wealth let alone have enough for retirement. They need <u>tax-FREE compounding</u>.

The following graph makes clear that in order to accumulate $1,000,000 from monthly contributions, we must buy and hold the securities of growing companies worldwide AND pay **zero** tax on the growth to ***maximize compounding***. We can see clearly that investing in growing company stocks is more likely to get us to our goal in our lifetime than investing in government bonds or a bank savings account. (lower lines)

As your investments grow—especially mutual funds that pay dividends and gains each year—you will not have to pay tax on them because of your special IRS-approved account. Most regular IRAs and pension accounts are tax-DEFERRED ***not*** tax-FREE. Taxes have to be paid sometime.

<u>Senator William Roth got us this account in 1998</u>. Your Roth IRA allows you to leverage tax-FREE accumulations over time against an immediate tax deduction as with a regular IRA or 401k pension. The benefits can be enormous: if you contributed $250 a month to your low-cost stock mutual funds, you could spend $30,000 tax-FREE for every $3,000 you deposited!

Invest $250 a month, $3000 a year, never pay tax

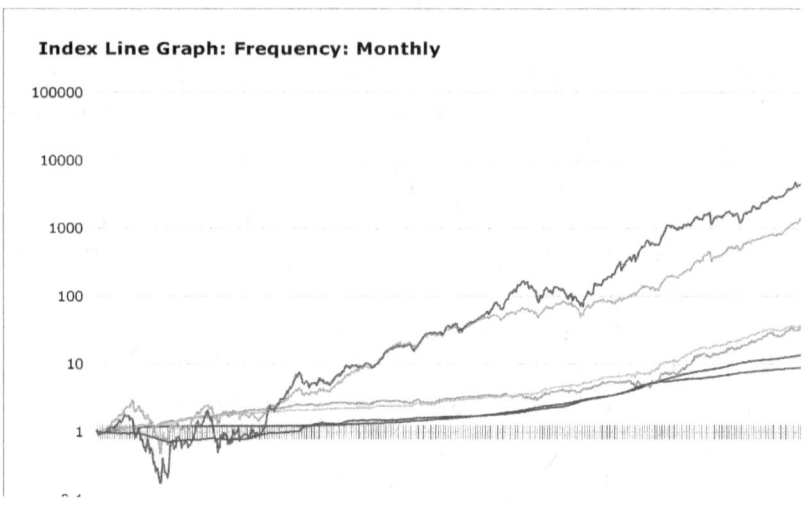

Index Line Graph: Frequency: Monthly

Top line—Small Cap Stocks
2nd line—Large Cap Stocks (S&P 500)
3rd line—US Long-term Corporate Bonds
4th line—Intermediate-term Government Bonds
5th line—US 30 day Government T-bills
6th line—US inflation
Courtesy: Dr. Campbell R. Harvey http://www.duke.edu/~charvey/

Tax-FREE v Taxable

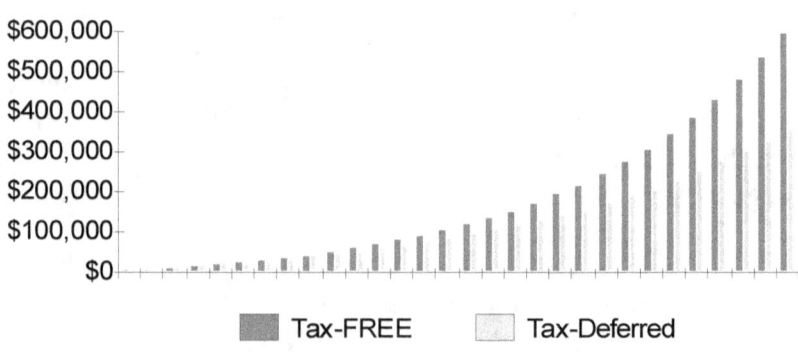

Tax-FREE   Tax-Deferred

The Roth IRA Rules

Contributions:

$5,500 ($6,500 over age 50) each year
Income under $135,000 (2018) single
married $199,000 (2018)

Distributions:

Tax-FREE for contributions.
And Tax-FREE for earnings if
Over age 591/2,
Account open 5 years,
Taxable earnings unless
Disabled,
First home ($10,000),
Death

Bonus:

Account can grow tax-FREE for life
Minimum distribution rules don't apply
Heirs don't pay income tax
Account has no maximum

Check with your tax preparer
https://www.irs.gov/pub/irs-pdf/p590a.pdf

Buffett's investment plan

You don't need an advisor. You can manage the rules of your Roth IRA account yourself. The rules are found at https://www.irs.gov/retirement-plans/roth-iras. Your account trustee can answer most questions. You don't need to pay an attorney. All of the large low-cost mutual funds firms are trustees. I will discuss the best firms available below.

You can start this account with any of the firms with no upfront charges. Most charge an annual fee for the bookkeeping. We will consider the specific investment options later. We will use low-cost firms because you will keep more of your own money. You save money when you don't pay Wall Street to 'advise' you.

It is important to pick a trustee with the least costs since over time the annual costs can really destroy your accumulations. For instance, if you use a brokerage firm, you might pay 2-3% of your balance annually. You could give up 63% of your earnings. If both spouses have a low-cost account with contributions of $250 a month for 27 years, they could accumulate $1,000,000. If they use a high-cost broker/advisor, both accounts may hit only $282,000. Depending on earnings of 8-10% and total costs of 2% per year, you could really hurt yourself. You need to watch the costs. Advisors do NOT beat the markets over the long term. Just stick with your One Decision plan.

You can open your account at any age as long as you have *earned* income—paper route too. Stock dividends or interest do not count. Any job will do. You don't even need a job requiring a W-2 to prove it. A part-time, weekend or night job will do. Any cash-only work will qualify—even for a child. Accountants recommend that receipts and records be maintained. You could even work for yourself in a home-office business like I do.

Nontaxable distributions from a Roth IRA won't affect your eligibility for student aid either. Later, in retirement, this money won't affect your social security benefits as of the rules today.

The *Miracle of Compounding* works.

Actual client Tom's account, investing $250 a month, 1962-2003

24%	3,720
16%	7,795
12%	12,091
-10%	13,582
24%	20,561
11%	26,153
-8%	26,821
4%	31,013
14%	38,775
19%	49,713
-14%	45,333
-26%	35,766
37%	53,110
24%	69,576
-8%	66,770
6%	73,956
18%	90,809
32%	123,827
-5%	120,486
22%	150,653
21%	185,920
6%	200,255
32%	268,297
19%	322,843
5%	342,135
17%	403,808
32%	536,987
-3%	523,787
31%	690,091
8%	748,538
10%	826,692
2%	846,286
38%	1,172,015
23%	1,445,268
33%	1,926,197
28%	2,469,372
21%	2,991,570
-9%	2,725,059
-12%	2,403,420
-22%	1,874,601
29%	2,412,905

13

Compound stock earnings

Compounding high earnings is your *best* strategy. The wealthy get richer just by leaving their money invested. They don't work more hours or take more risks. The famous 1% at the top of society take down 23.5% of all income (up from 8.9% 30 years ago). They don't work any harder than you do—*their money does*.

Because of compounding, many millionaires have said, "the first million was the hardest." It takes a working business person about 34 years to grow $250 a month to $1,000,000 using tax-advantaged investments. However, it only takes 7-9 years to double their money to $2 million. Investors in stock funds, earning 10-12% on average, can double it again to $4 million in less than 10 years without adding new money. Their tax-advantaged accounts make it easier to reach their goal. It is compounding that makes it happen—not Wall Street 'advice' for the fees.

Compounding of high earnings means that we make money on our last period's accumulations. The progression looks like the client's account values on the previous page. Notice that our balance can double in a couple of good years. This happens because we are adding up to 38% of the previous year's balance not because we add $3,000. We are making money on top of our money with no extra effort on our part. During this 40 year period, this client 'lost' share value some years. In fact, they lost 14% and then 26% back to back, but then made 37% and 24%.

Wealthy people don't panic. They have learned that compounding over the long-term is the only way they can build wealth. There are no successful get-rich-quick schemes for the investors. To reach their goal, they know there will be setbacks. No business grows steadily upward all the time. They have seen the losses before and they don't sell their assets in a panic.

We will buy assets that "grow by themselves." We will have security because our ***purchasing power*** will grow over time. We begin with a fund with 500 large company stocks. We earn 10-12%. Some go on to buy all ten Vanguard funds reducing the market ups and downs. We still buy the shares because their value goes up over time. We buy the shares monthly and *the number of our shares* never *goes down*.

The Vanguard Top Ten

2017 Total Return	Fund	Long-term Return	Longevity
21.7%	*500 Index*	*11.1%**	*since 1976*
3.2%	Energy	10.7%	since 1984
17.9%	Extended Market	10.9%	since 1987
19.6%	Health	16.5%	since 1984
42.9%	International Growth	10.8%	since 1981
29.5%	PRIMECAP	13.9%	since 1984
16.1%	Small Cap Index	10.7%	since 1960
10.2%	Wellesley Income	9.9%	since 1970
19.1%	Windsor	11.5%	since 1958
16.8%	Windsor II	10.8%	since 1985
19.7%	Average	11.7%	

*Average Annual Returns as of 12/31/17.

This kind of security comes from our regular contributions ... and patience. The miracle of compounding works its magic on the fund shares when we give it TIME. The wealthy give their **assets** time to compound. They don't take them out and they try not to pay tax every year on the gains. They maintain their contribution schedule because each $100 added is worth $1,000 to them later. They use the compound interest calculator so they know the future value: moneychimp.com/calculator/compound_interest_calculator.htm.

Most people who become wealthy have to wait for years of slow growth in their account. It took client Tom 21 years to get to $150,000. Then it took only 14 years to get to a $1,172,015. After only 4 years, it became $3,000,000. Shortly thereafter he "lost" over a million dollars! He never lost his shares since he never sold.

This client stuck with it and was successful in reaching the goal but there are many who do not. Most people who are not wealthy already, have a hard time believing it can happen with only their *patience*. They just don't have the experience of how compounding works to keep faith in its outcome eventually.

Once an account becomes sizable, we don't need to add contributions to it--usually, by the time we stop regular employment. Some people continue to work after age 65 because they love what they do and want to continue. Obviously, they don't need to work. The **miracle of compounding** does the work then.

The annual returns of growing companies

2016 Total Return	Fund	Long-term Return	Longevity
11.9%	500 Index	10.9%*	since 1976
33.1%	Energy	10.9%	since 1984
16.1%	Extended Market	10.7%	since 1987
-9.0%	Health	16.4%	since 1984
1.7%	International Growth	10.0%	since 1981
10.7%	PRIMECAP	13.4%	since 1984
18.3%	Small Cap Index	10.7%	since 1960
8.1%	Wellesley Income	9.9%	since 1970
12.5%	Windsor	11.3%	since 1958
13.4%	Windsor II	10.7%	since 1985
11.7%	Average	11.5%	

*Average Annual Returns as of 12/31/16.

Range of annual returns of stocks, 1950 – 2000

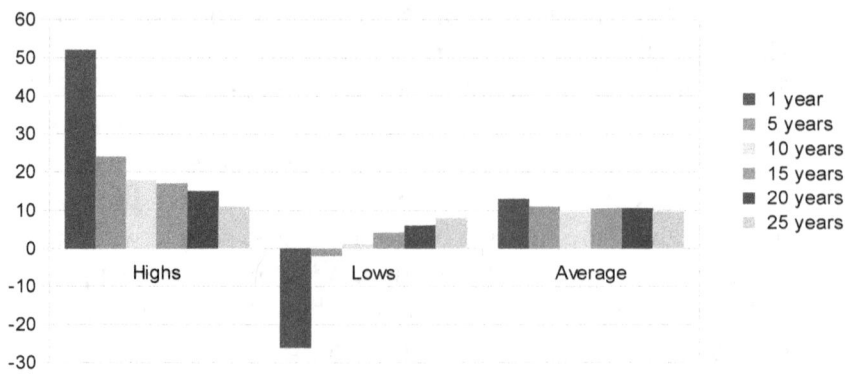

16

Buy buy buy investing

When we develop the ***habit*** of investing, we take our emotions out of the process. We, as a silent partner, must learn to live with the market downs. We need to think of this account as our stake in growing businesses as the number of shares grow. See page 13.

It is easier to be patient if we make contributions automatic. Like the Social Security contributions we make every payday, the contributions come out of our bank automatically. We can have the Roth IRA trustee debit our checking account automatically every month. Businesses grow in spurts. We must hold on to our *shares*.

As one client told us, "I never see the deduction, so I never miss it." Of course this client has already identified the $250 he has committed to his $1,000,000 future. He took our advice and went through his spending on financial services. He used our Guides to find the $250 a month he was wasting on products and services he would never use or need. In our amazon.com/Insiders-Guides-Discount-Financial-Services/ you will find **"tricks of the trade"** that we insiders use to buy directly from high quality manufacturers for less.

It's easy to say **I will start later**. Starting 5 years later means ending up with HALF the amount we were shooting for. It is hard to believe that missing that $250 a month for 5 years or $15,000 can reduce our total from $600,000 to $300,000.

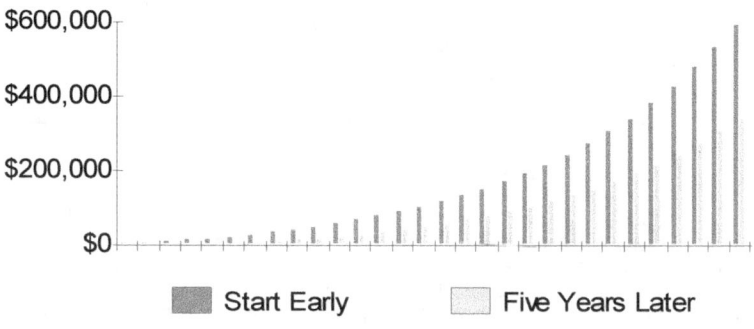

The Value of Starting Early

Your investment plan over time

$2,000 Annual Stock Market Investment 1950- '70- '80- '90- 2013

Year	Returns	Balance	Balance	Balance	Balance	Balance
		$2,000				
1950	31%	$2,620				
1951	24%	$5,729				
1952	18%	$9,120				
1953	-1%	$11,009				
1954	52%	$19,773				
1955	31%	$28,523				
1956	5%	$32,049				
1957	-11%	$30,304				
1958	43%	$46,194				
1959	12%	$53,978				
1960	1%	$56,538				
1961	26%	$73,757				
1962	-8%	$69,697				
1963	24%	$88,904				
1964	16%	$105,449				
1965	12%	$120,342				
1966	-10%	$110,108				
1967	24%	$139,014				
1968	11%	$156,526				
1969	-8%	$145,844	2,000			
1970	4%	$153,757	2,080			
1971	14%	$177,563	4,651			
1972	19%	$213,681	7,915			
1973	-14%	$185,485	8,527			
1974	-26%	$138,739	7,790			
1975	37%	$192,813	13,412			
1976	24%	$241,568	19,111			
1977	-8%	$224,082	19,422			
1978	6%	$239,647	22,707			
1979	18%	$285,144	29,155	2,000		
1980	32%	$379,030	41,124	2,640		
1981	-5%	$361,978	40,968	4,408		
1982	22%	$444,053	52,421	7,818		
1983	21%	$539,724	65,850	11,879		
1984	6%	$574,228	71,921	14,712		
1985	32%	$760,621	97,575	22,060		
1986	19%	$907,519	118,494	28,632		
1987	5%	$954,995	126,519	32,163		
1988	17%	$1,119,684	150,367	39,971		
1989	32%	$1,480,623	201,125	55,402	2,000	
1990	-3%	$1,438,144	197,031	55,680	1,940	
1991	31%	$1,886,589	260,731	75,560	5,161	
1992	8%	$2,039,676	283,749	83,765	7,734	
1993	10%	$2,245,843	314,324	94,342	10,708	
1994	2%	$2,292,800	322,651	98,268	12,962	
1995	38%	$3,166,824	448,018	138,370	20,647	
1996	23%	$3,897,654	553,522	172,656	27,856	
1997	33%	$5,186,540	738,844	232,292	39,709	
1998	28%	$6,641,331	948,281	299,894	53,387	
1999	21%	$8,038,430	1,149,839	365,291	67,019	
2000	-9%	$7,316,791	1,048,174	334,235	62,807	
2001	-12%	$6,447,855	925,203	296,223	57,095	
2002	-22%	$5,024,437	722,291	232,316	46,035	
2003	29%	$6,459,474	930,787	301,119	61,730	
2004	11%	$7,164,483	1,034,274	336,099	70,664	
2005	5%	$7,512,677	1,084,540	352,433	74,098	
2006	15%	$8,694,884	1,259,259	412,409	90,450	
2007	5%	$9,163,538	1,327,133	434,638	95,325	
2008	-39%	$5,601,431	813,388	268,074	60,754	
2009	27%	$7,116,358	952,155	342,993	79,699	
2010	15%	$8,186,112	1,097,278	396,742	93,954	
2011	2%	$8,347,378	1,118,894	404,558	95,805	
2012	16%	$9,666,264	1,295,679	468,478	110,942	
2013	32%	$12,759,468	1,710,296	618,390	146,443	
Avg.	12%	12%	11%	13%	11%	

Ibbotson Associates **Stocks average 11.4% per year, bonds 5%, CDs 3%.** Stocks have gone up as much as 54% and as low as –43% in 1 year, up to 28% or down to –12% in 5 years, up 20% or down 0% in 10 years, up 18% or up 3% in 20 years. Short term bonds have gone up 14% or up 0% in 1 year, up 11% or up 0% in 5 years, up 9% or up 0% in 10 years, up 10% or up 1% in 20 years.

18

Avoid "high-fee managers"

**"In every single time period and data point tested,
low-cost funds beat high-cost funds."**

According to an unbiased <u>Morningstar</u> study, low-cost funds beat
high-cost funds, PERIOD. However, the myth of Wall Street is that
you must pay more for good performance. Warren Buffett's mentor,
Benjamin Graham, advised: "buy financial products like we buy
"<u>groceries, ... not perfume</u>."

The best predictor of your investing and wealth-building
success is **low cost**. When we subtract the costs of buying and
maintaining investments, we give up a lot of the gains. A stock
fund that reflects the overall market is called an index fund. This
kind of fund costs only <u>0.04%</u> ($4 per $10,000). Our account will
compound at or near the 10-12% trend over time.

The chart below makes it clear. Over time, the advisor costs
we pay each year will cut our total accumulation by up to 63%.
Instead of compounding at 10-12% annually on average, some
people give up 1.5-3% of the earnings on their money to the
middle person. They end up with less.

Low-cost index funds beat <u>95%</u> of funds with a stock-picking
manager. Wall Street takes <u>$ 1.3 Trillion of our money in fees</u>.

Liar's Club: 'I can beat the market'

Liar's Poker is a game author Michael Lewis says traders play when they get bored. It involves bluffing. But when your advisor or money manager does it to you, it's fraud. When retail customers don't know how and where to invest properly, sales people make up stories. They don't lie exactly; they mislead. Sales people only survive if they separate you from your money or your potential earnings. Fact: You need a plan that takes only one hour to follow.

Picking *individual* stocks as a strategy is not likely to work for us. Professional managers and day traders have had limited success over time. Our strategy is to build wealth as a silent partner in growing global companies. Since it is unlikely that we (or anyone else) will be able to pick the next Google or Apple, we invest in a large group of firms. We do not need to fear picking the wrong one or picking one at the wrong time. As the founder of the largest mutual fund firm, John Bogle, says: "Don't look for the needle. Buy the haystack." This is a proven successful strategy.

A mutual fund manager advertises that their fund has "beaten" the market and so we pay 1.5-3% of our assets every year. Over time we find that while the stock market index rose **11.06%**, we earned only **3.79%** annually. In this way, costs can take 63% of our returns over time. Each time they sell and buy, we give up some of our compound earnings. Plus we pay fees and taxes.

When young investors begin investing, they cannot buy all 10 Vanguard funds listed above at once with $250 per month. Vanguard has minimums on all funds so they can keep their expenses low for everyone.

There are two ways to start our Roth IRA account. The easiest way is to save $250 a month in our savings account until we have the $1,000 minimum for Vanguard's entry fund: STAR #56. We can open the Roth IRA by phone or online: STAR minimum is $1,000. Most Vanguard funds need $3,000 to start. We can keep contributing to the STAR fund until we have $3,000 for the 500 Index and then $3,000 for the Extended Market funds and eventually all 10 funds. Vanguard is at 800.551.8631.

The second way to begin is to open a Roth IRA at TIAA, the world's largest pension company, primarily for educational and research institutions. Low expenses and low initial contributions make TIAA an organization we can stay with. TIAA 800.842.2888.

At TIAA we can make application and begin immediately with an automatic monthly contribution of $100 or more from our bank account. We can follow how the assets grow by themselves. TIAA has two funds that provide us with the diversity of companies worldwide: TIAA Equity Index and TIAA International Equity.

Request a prospectus (owner's manual) for each fund you will be using at Vanguard or TIAA. Both mutual fund firms have experienced salaried representatives that provide accurate information about accounts and funds. Both offer low-cost index funds that hold a broad representation of the market returns of 10-12%. This is a building block to accumulating wealth.

Both firms are focused on you, not on profits.

Our strategy is to buy mutual funds with stocks of growing companies worldwide. No Wall Street guru can predict the future winners. Most can't do better than 50%—a flip of the coin. Your investments provide long-term growth of 10-12% annually on average with the benefit of avoiding single company or industry failures. It provides exposure to new growth potential around the world with less risk than holding one company, one sector, or one country. Some years our account is up 33% and some years down 22%. However, we double our money every 7-9 years *over time.*

How does your investment grow? Time is the key. Take as example your payday contributions to Social Security. A couple pays in 6.2% of salary. It is matched by the employer. Baby Boomers who made average salaries all their lives are now taking benefits of about $1,500 each--$36,000 a year. Because benefits are pegged to inflation, they may receive $1,260,000 during the rest of their lives. However, SS contributions are NOT invested in the stock market index.

Our investments earn 10-12% a year in an index earning much more than SS contributions. It is TIME that makes wealth.

It is the amount we KEEP that matters!

Monthly	Accumulation at 12% per year									
	5	10	15	20	25	30	35	40	45	50
$100	$8,167	$23,004	$49,958	$98,925	$187,884	$349,496	$643,095	$1,176,477	$2,145,469	$3,905,834
$200	$16,334	$46,008	$99,916	$197,850	$375,768	$698,992	$1,286,190	$2,352,954	$4,290,938	$7,811,668
$300	$24,501	$69,012	$149,874	$296,775	$563,652	$1,048,488	$1,929,285	$3,529,431	$6,436,408	$11,717,502
$500	$40,835	$115,020	$249,790	$494,625	$939,420	$1,747,480	$3,215,475	$5,882,385	$10,727,346	$19,529,169

. . .

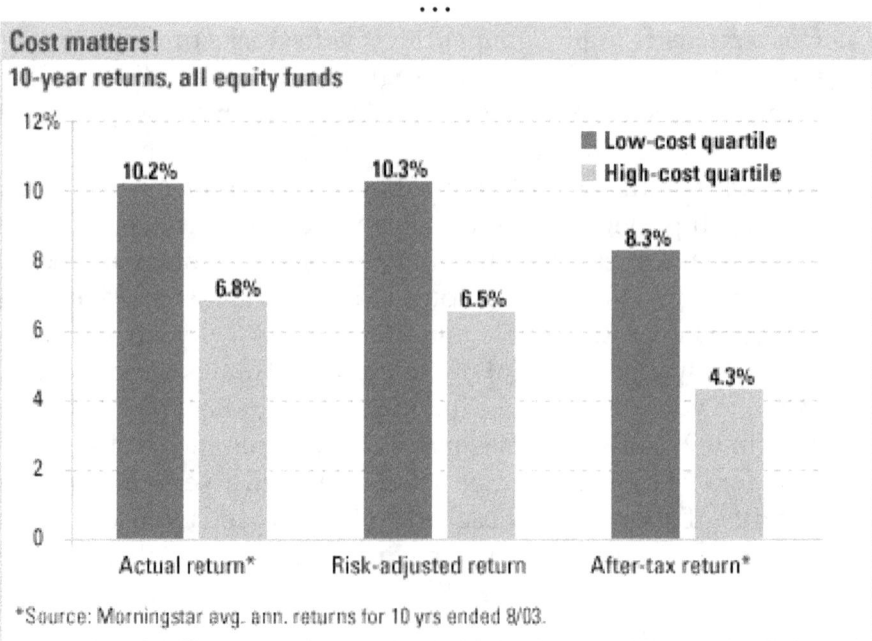

Cost matters!
10-year returns, all equity funds

- ■ Low-cost quartile
- ■ High-cost quartile

Actual return*: 10.2% / 6.8%
Risk-adjusted return: 10.3% / 6.5%
After-tax return*: 8.3% / 4.3%

*Source: Morningstar avg. ann. returns for 10 yrs ended 8/03.

22

Invest every month automatically

We need to find at least $250 per month to invest in order to build our account. We can build wealth by following the strategy outlined in the previous chapters, but we need to have at least 10% of income available to invest. In my experience, it doesn't matter how much people earn, most say they don't have the money to invest for their future. "Today is hard enough," they complain.

Yes, that may well be, but if we don't find the $250, for example, we won't have a very happy tomorrow. We have to go back to our goal. We want to build wealth: accumulating $1,000,000 over time. Based on the way wealth compounds, we need to invest at least $250 a month, every month. We need to be consistent for the **miracle of compounding** to work.

A Spending Plan is a way to set priorities for our regular spending. We can accumulate $1 million to accomplish all that we want to do in life by using just 10 percent of our income to buy assets that "grow by themselves." We don't run the firms we own.

Using a Spending Plan is **like brushing your teeth**—it's a habit that isn't that difficult to learn—then it is automatic. Our Spending Plan must include what we need to function now and in the future. Like building a business, it takes planning and following the steps we talked about so far.

Some investors include the $250 in their automatic bill payment or have the trustee debit their account automatically. Others set up family goals and decide to put a certain amount in a separate account for each goal. In this way, they keep the wealth building process in the forefront of their monthly bill payments.

Whatever way works for you. The important thing is to change the status of wealth building from a vague future desire to a monthly habit. "Set it and forget it" is the theme of investing.

Most people find that the easiest way is to set up an automatic debit of their checking account by the trustee at the time of the application for the Roth IRA. If we are using a Roth 401k or an employer account, we set up the retirement account with automatic contributions. We are less likely to quit if a trustee debits monthly.

Some people are successful by making a written plan. They

have some idea of how much they will need at some time in the future. The account is set up as a Roth IRA so the **contributions** are not taxed when used before age 59.5. After that age, there are no taxes at all—EVER.

Another benefit of using a Spending Plan is that we become focused on how we spend our money. We are more inclined to buy only what we need. For financial services, we 'insiders' compiled the **_The Insiders Guides_** for each area—insurance, securities, etc. They provide an easy way to save $3,000 or more on financial products we already use. This is where we buy discount products.

We can't build wealth by spending more than we earn. Building wealth takes patience and commitment to contributing to our investment business every month. Some people don't try to be disciplined investors. They let the trustee debit the $250 or 10% every month so they can't fail to become a millionaire.

Are you paying too much?

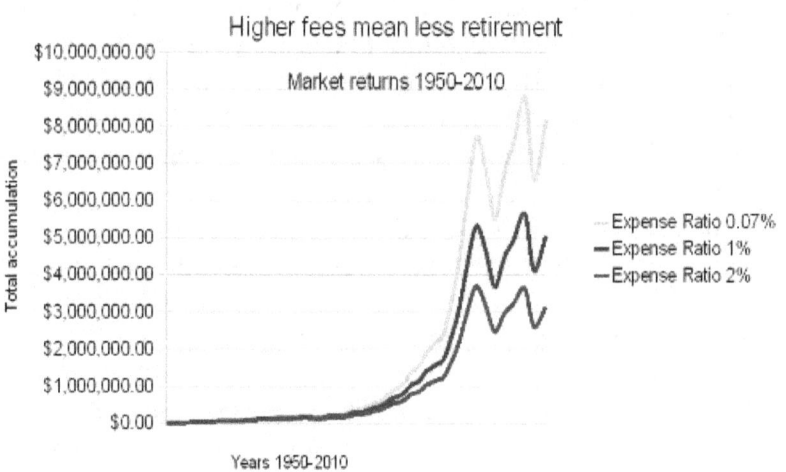

Higher fees mean less retirement

Market returns 1950-2010

- Expense Ratio 0.07%
- Expense Ratio 1%
- Expense Ratio 2%

Years 1950-2010

Buy low-cost financial products

John Bogle invented the low-cost mutual fund cooperative structure that allows us to accumulate stock earnings at cost—No middle person or profit firm to take a large chunk of our earnings. It is not picking stocks but *time* that builds wealth.   It is easy to build wealth if we already have a pile of money. But how do we capture that first $500,000, that $250,000, or even that first $50,000? It comes from buying assets that 'grow by themselves.' It takes time for the companies we own through your fund to produce earnings. As <u>Buffett just proved</u>, the easiest way to make sure we reach our goal of a million dollars is to buy low-cost.

But where do we get the $250 a month? The best way is to "REDIRECT" the **cash we already spend** on things we really don't need or can buy for less. This is how millionaires stay millionaires. They don't over pay!

Most working people waste $3,000 or more each year on financial services. We must shop for financials like we shop for groceries: buy the house brand and use discounts. For instance, the difference between paying full price for a new car and a 3-year-old model can be 40% or more.

Buy for every financial need for less:

Auto insurance: save $400 or more EVERY year by changing/ dropping some benefits we don't need.

Home insurance: save $200 or more EVERY year by changing one limit.

Life insurance: save $1,000 or more EVERY year by using direct to consumer term insurer.

Mutual funds: save $2-3,000 EVERY year by using low-cost providers.

Bank: save $120 EVERY year by using a low-cost provider of the benefits we usually use. Credit Union.

Mortgage: save $2,000 on closings and lower interest rates.

Investments: earn 15-30% *guaranteed* just by paying off credit cards.

Low-cost mutual funds: save up to 63% over time.

Tax refund: Averages $3,022 and usually spent.

Using our *The Insiders' Guides to Buying Discount Financial Services: Buy Direct and Save $3,000 Every Year,* we can redirect $250 a month without having to give up anything. We don't need to tighten our belt or make a budget. We can give up things we would not benefit from anyway.

Best example: MetLife charged $983 for a $300,000 30-year **term policy**. This same $300,000 benefit was sold by Savings Bank Life Insurance for $384 a year. Their financial strength ratings are A+ and their underwriting requirements are the same. The difference, $599, over 30 years is $17,970. If invested, this difference can add $175,000 to OUR **account**.

This strategy—to cut out the middle people who are taking our money with little benefit to us—makes sense and works! But the most important part of our strategy is keep investing: *buying more shares of mutual funds when they are 'on sale.'*

2011 Total Return	Fund	Long-term Return*	Longevity
1.97%	500 Index	10.36%	since 1976
-1.74%	Energy	12.71%	since 1984
-3.73%	Extended Market	9.96%	since 1987
11.45%	Health	16.30%	since 1984
-13.68%	International Growth	10.50%	since 1981
-1.84%	PRIMECAP	12.79%	since 1984
-2.80%	Small Cap Index	10.26%	since 1960
9.63%	Wellesley Income	10.16%	since 1970
-4.00%	Windsor	11.00%	since 1958
2.70%	Windsor II	10.18%	since 1985
0.00%	Average	11.42%	

*Average Annual Returns as of 12/31/11.

We must ignore what others are doing when some markets fall because we are gaining more shares NOT cashing in at panic prices. Just remember George Bailey's talk during the 1929 panic:

Potter isn't selling. Potter's buying! And why? Because we're panicky and he's not. That's why. He's pickin' up some bargain. Now, we can get through this thing all right. We've, we've got to stick together, though. We've got to have faith in each other. *It's a Wonderful Life*

Manage investments once a year

"We continue to make more money when *snoring* than when active."

Warren Buffett gave us this advice. As the most successful investor of our day we should listen. He is making it clear that we should NOT touch our investments very often. We buy shares of the top companies and hold them all our lives—selling them only for our retirement income.

Wall Street makes money on transactions. So don't trade. We ignore the market and keep buying so we end up with $1 million. When the market is down we keep our mind on the graph on p. 17. We have to remember Warren Buffett's advice and hold on to stocks/stock funds. In fact, Mr Buffett says "**our favorite holding period is forever.**" http://www.berkshirehathaway.com/letters/1988.html

Even if the market drops; it will rise. It fell 22% in 2002 and rose 29% in 2003. We only have to look at our tax-FREE account once a year. We make sure we are making contributions to the specific mutual fund that is down for the year. We don't 'rebalance.'

When we first started investing, we use the STAR Index. After we had accumulated enough to buy the 500 Index ($3,000), we trade shares of the STAR Index and buy it. We keep investing into the 500 Index until we have the minimum for the next one. We repeat this pattern until we have the minimum in each. Then we add to the one that is down for the year. Repeat each year.

As we accumulate the minimum for each fund, then transfer into the next one, we do not need to pay tax on the sale because we are using a tax-FREE Roth IRA. This is part of the **miracle of compounding**. After accumulating a large proportion of our goal, adding the $250 per month does not matter to the outcome. We can borrow to pay for cars, vacation, other goals. For instance, our client whose account is shown on page 13 took $25,000 for a used luxury car in the year the account hit over half a million. His account total did not suffer long term.

Managing investments once a year is wise advice. Our tax-FREE account does not require us to hire an advisor to manage it.

We have the *power of compounding* so we don't need advisors.

Plan spending wisely

We own the 10 funds to build wealth. We have learned to be patient and accumulate $1,000,000 or more. We have paid back any amounts that we borrowed to pay cash for large purchases. We have been fortunate that the historical averages of market returns have produced the accumulations we set as our goals.

NOW WHAT?

Now we can take 6-8% out of the account each year and pay no income taxes. As of 2018, most states follow the IRS code on our **account**, a Roth IRA. https://www.irs.gov/retirement-plans/roth-iras

Many people move 60% of their money into a balanced fund like the Wellesley Income fund. It has produced over 9% per year on average since 1970. They created a retirement spending plan that assured them of that monthly income of a fixed dollar amount with this Guide. amazon.com/Your-Retirement-Spending-Plan-enough.

We have created our $1,000,000 nest egg in order to provide the same buying power as we have today because of inflation. I am assuming that most working families will need at least $50,000 a year to live on in retirement. We don't know what will happen to Social Security by 2034. We don't know what employer pensions might look like by then. I am assuming that inflation will continue so planning is crucial to success in retirement.

Inflation will make the goods we buy now for $50,000 cost about $80,000. If Social Security or employer pensions can add to our basic income, that is fine. But we don't want to count on them. If there is a bad year like 2008, we are not taking money out of our growth funds at a bad time. The balanced fund has bonds which have traditionally been less volatile.

The funds we have listed above include some of the most consistent low volatility returns over time. Since our account is not taxable, there are no taxes when we take our monthly income later. We may not have to pay tax on our other income like Social Security and/or our qualified retirement funds. The gains on our account are tax-FREE after age 59.5. Unlike pensions and annuities, this account is tax-FREE. We pay $99,000 ($3,000 for 33 years) and $901,000 is FREE of tax.

The Keys to Wealth

1. **Costs matter**: Broker/advisor cost 1% to 3% every year

   If you use a salesperson, costs take HALF your money!
   $3,000 per year @11%   for 33 years = $1,018,177
   $3,000 per year @11-1% for 33 years = $778,768
   $3,000 per year @11-2% for 33 years = $613,805
   $3,000 per year @11-3% for 33 years = $486,634
   www.moneychimp.com/calculator/compound_interest_calculator.htm

2.   Broker/advisor stock-picking does not beat index funds over time. No money manager has been able to beat the markets consistently. No one can forecast the future. http://investa.com/man-vs-machine-the-great-stock-showdown-wall-street-journal-05-10-13/

3. **Compounding** creates investment success; NOT buying and selling. The chance of you doing both, at the right times, is near zero. Warren Buffett's holding period is "forever." No trading!

4. A **tax-FREE** investment account increases your balance 30%.

5. Putting all your money in one stock or market sector guarantees failure over time. No one investment is perfect. Buy a **group of growing global businesses in a low-cost fund.**

6.   '**Dollar cost average**' buying technique lowers the cost of shares over time. When you invest a fixed amount each month, you buy more mutual fund shares when the price is low and less when high. Over time, you will own more shares at a lower average cost.

7.   **Consistency** wins over the long term. Quick in and out trading only benefits Wall Street. Market timing may work for a short time but the odds of being right on the buy and sell are long.

8.   **Patience** is required to allow your money to work for you. Building a business takes time. Investing is betting to most of us.

One Decision is all we need

With **One Decision**, we can earn 11% on our long-term money and end up with a million dollars or more with one phone call. Now you see how to accumulate more by NOT paying for help you don't need. John Bogle, Warren Buffett and William Roth have provided the way to grow our wealth with **no tax and at cost**. We can now complete an excellent financial plan in 1 hour. We can now earn 10-12% vs. 3.79% on our money. We can now use a proven LONG-TERM strategy so we take advantage of the most powerful investing force—compounding.

Bogle proved cost matters. Buffett proved a simple market index beat the best Wall Street 'fortune tellers.' Sen Roth helped us avoid taxes like the rich. Compounding our assets is the key to wealth not salespeople. Loaning money to a business over time so you can claim part of the profits is how the rich get and **stay** rich. Extra work is not necessary if we use the **One Decision** way.

Fidelity found that the **most successful investors** were those that forgot their account or died. Most wealthy investors have learned patience is the Buffett secret to investing. They see how **costs destroy** their portfolio compounding. They avoid sales hype and use the strategy discussed above. That is why they stay rich.

The industry has made building wealth a mystery so it can take $1.3 Trillion from our accounts year after year. The average advisor-run account return was only 3.79%. The fees buy toys for the Pimps of Wall Street. Over time that fee compounds our loss and can take up to 63% of our total possible accumulations. Advisors like to buy and sell creating fees for them; taxes for us.

Advisors charge 1-3% whether they beat the averages or not. Advisors don't give refunds! The clear winning strategy is to use one or 10 funds and let compounding work its magic. Over time using a tax-FREE account with low fees, we can accumulate $1,000,000 from $250 a month at 10-12%. Using this calculator moneychimp.com/calculator/compound_interest_calculator.htm, we find the range is 31 to 35 years. If our spouse has an account, we can shorten the time to 26-29 years for a family $1 million.

If we use an advisor, we may give up over $500,000 in total accumulations. Research has shown that the average investor actually earns just <u>3.79% not 11%</u> annually over time.

Our funds for building wealth work because they are low-cost strategies inside a unique **tax-FREE trust account.** This eliminates the biggest killers of wealth: TAXES and FEES. We can be our own masters of tax-FREE wealth with patience. There is no need to pick stocks or hire expensive advisors or product pushers with hidden fees. We can do it ourselves as long as we have a plan. The plan is <u>following Warren Buffett's strategy</u>.

One Decision investing is up to you. Advisors can't profit from these steps so you have to call Vanguard or TIAA *yourself* to set up your account. It takes about 1 hour to set up a Roth IRA for each of you. You can do it online or by phone. You can begin with TIAA and $100 automatic contributions or Vanguard with $1,000. Put the contributions on automatic so you don't have to decide every month whether to invest. Future life happens and you want to be spending your $60-80,000 a year not praying Washington won't <u>cut Social Security benefits</u> every year.

If you have been investing, you can convert portions of your IRA each year, paying tax on the earnings as you go. Over time, your Roth account will grow with earnings that are tax-FREE. This money may reduce your overall tax in retirement. It also is a great estate planning tool since no tax will be due from your heirs either.

There is a clear reason why "working millionaires" become wealthy. It is not luck or inheritance. Millions of immigrants to this country have done it before. They lived below their means. They saved and invested in businesses. They did not let temporary cash flow problems stop them from building wealth. They accumulated hard assets and shares of companies and mutual funds.

As many clients say, "I never even miss the contributions because I never see them. Then all of a sudden, I see my statement has $25,000, $50,000, $250,000, $1,000,000, $2,000,000. We are talking real money here."

The real secret to investing is **<u>compounding</u>**. Buffett says:

"My wealth has come from a combination of living in America, some lucky genes, and
compound interest."

Call Vanguard **800-551-8631** or TIAA **800-223-1200** today.

The Author

Law Steeple has been in financial services for over 20 years. He was a managing executive of the sales units of a number of bank securities firms. He is the author of *Tax-FREE Wealth: How to use the tax laws for $2,000,000 free of tax*. He is one of the insiders who contributed to the The Insiders Guides set of buyers' guides edited by Dan Keppel. The guides provide specific ways to save on all financial services. Law lives in New Jersey and Florida.

The Insiders' Guides to Buying Discount Financial Services: Buy Direct and Save $3,000 Every Year is available at Amazon, Barnes & Noble, Junglee, bookadda, allbookstores, ebay, fishpond, alibris, powells, booksamillion, etc

To receive Dan Keppel's weekly Alert, go to www.TheInsidersGuides.com

The Miracle of Compounding

The best argument we've seen for teaching about finance and the power of compounding is summed up by the table below. These figures are based on an assumed annual rate of return of 10 percent, with no withdrawals and no taxes.

Age	Example 1: Annual Investment	Year-End Value	Example 2: Annual Investment	Year-End Value
19	$ 2,000	$2,200	$ 0	$ 0
20	$ 2,000	$4,620	$ 0	$ 0
21	$ 2,000	$7,282	$ 0	$ 0
22	$ 2,000	$10,210	$ 0	$ 0
23	$ 2,000	$13,431	$ 0	$ 0
24	$ 2,000	$ 16,974	$ 0	$ 0
25	$ 2,000	$ 20,872	$ 0	$ 0
26	$ 2,000	$ 25,159	$ 0	$ 0
27	$ 0	$ 27,675	$2,000	$2,200
28	$ 0	$ 30,442	$2,000	$4,620
29	$ 0	$33,487	$2,000	$7,282
30	$ 0	$36,835	$2,000	$10,210
31	$ 0	$40,519	$2,000	$13,431
32	$ 0	$44,571	$2,000	$16,974
33	$ 0	$49,028	$2,000	$20,872

34	$ 0	$53,931	$2,000	$25,159
35	$ 0	$59,324	$2,000	$29,875
36	$ 0	$65,256	$2,000	$35,062
37	$ 0	$71,782	$2,000	$40,769
38	$ 0	$78,960	$2,000	$47,045
39	$ 0	$86,856	$2,000	$53,950
40	$ 0	$95,541	$2,000	$61,545
41	$ 0	$105,095	$2,000	$69,899
42	$ 0	$115,605	$2,000	$79,089
43	$ 0	$127,165	$2,000	$89,198
44	$ 0	$139,882	$2,000	$100,318
45	$ 0	$153,870	$2,000	$112,550
46	$ 0	$169,257	$2,000	$126,005
47	$ 0	$186,183	$2,000	$140,805
48	$ 0	$204,801	$2,000	$157,086
49	$ 0	$225,281	$2,000	$174,995
50	$ 0	$247,809	$2,000	$194,694
51	$ 0	$272,590	$2,000	$216,364
52	$ 0	$299,849	$2,000	$240,200
53	$ 0	$329,834	$2,000	$266,420
54	$ 0	$362,818	$2,000	$295,262

55	$ 0	$399,100	$2,000	$326,988
56	$ 0	$439,010	$2,000	$361,887
57	$ 0	$482,910	$2,000	$400,276
58	$ 0	$531,202	$2,000	$442,503
59	$ 0	$584,322	$2,000	$488,953
60	$ 0	$642,754	$2,000	$540,049
61	$ 0	$707,029	$2,000	$596,254
62	$ 0	$777,732	$2,000	$658,079
63	$ 0	$855,505	$2,000	$726,087
64	$ 0	$941,056	$2,000	$800,896
65	$ 0	**$1,035,161**	$,2000	**$883,185**
Less $ invested		($16,000)		($78,000)
		$1,019,161		**$805,185**
Money increased		**64 fold**		**10 fold**

http://www.saferchild.org/power/ It is time not timing markets: Everyone has their time.

www.ingramcontent.com/pod-product-compliance
Lightning Source LLC
Chambersburg PA
CBHW071159220526
45468CB00003B/1086